Advice for parents

This *Practice Workbook* is designed to help y___
their learning and practise key problem solvin___
page is packed with questions and exercises ___
your child will cover in school.

The book is designed for children to complete on their own, but you may like to work with them for the first few pages to check they are happy with reading the questions. They can work through the book unit by unit, or can dip in and out to practise a particular skill.

The *Practice Workbook* range is easy to use as stand-alone workbooks. They also complement the *Practice* series, which is full of explanations and examples. If your child is finding something tricky, you may like to look at the corresponding *Practice* title to help unlock their understanding.

This book covers all the mathematical concepts taught in Years 3 and 4 at school. These are:

- Place value
- Fractions
- Decimals
- Addition and subtraction
- Money
- Measures: time, length, mass and capacity
- Puzzles
- Patterns and sequences
- Multiplication and division
- 2D and 3D shapes
- Position and directions
- Data handling

There are practice exercises to help keep the skills needed to problem solve fresh in the children's minds and problems to solve which involve using these skills.

> The children are likely to need to work out the solutions to the questions and problems on paper. This symbol ▤ indicates when this is appropriate. On these occasions the children should be encouraged to show their strategies.

1: Place value

Activity 1

Place these numbers on the number lines and then round them to the nearest 10 and nearest 100.

134

```
┌──────────────────┼──────────────────┐
100                                    200
```

134 to the nearest 10 = 130   134 to the nearest 100 = 100

298

```
┌──────────────────────────────────────┐
200                                    300
```

298 to the nearest 10 = 300   298 to the nearest 100 = 300

354

```
┌──────────────────────────────────────┐
300                                    400
```

354 to the nearest 10 = 350   354 to the nearest 100 = 400

Activity 2

Estimate the answers to these calculations by rounding the numbers to the nearest 10.

Then find out the actual answer and see how close you were.

a 89 + 72   Estimate: 160   How close? 11
Actual: 161

b 91 − 37   Estimate: 50   How close? 4
Actual: 54

c 134 + 128   Estimate: 260   How close? 2
Actual: 262

d 156 − 103   Estimate: 60   How close? 7
Actual: 53

89
72

4

Circle the hundreds digit in these numbers.

a 12 456   **b** 198   **c** 134 527   **d** 2476   **e** 875

Circle the tens digit in these numbers.

a 15 268   **b** 23 452   **c** 578   **d** 152   **e** 2469

What is the value of the 1 in these numbers?

a 2134 _Hund_

b 1459 _th_

c 12 495 _____

d 25 431 _____

e 24 218 _____

What number is 10 more than:

a 5286 _____

b 18 198 _____

c 4875 _____

d 6293 _____

e 14 173 _____

f 21 891 _____

g 2992 _____

Activity 7

What number is 3000 less than:

a 12 453 _____

b 23 897 _____

c 31 254 _____

d 11 842 _____

Activity 8

What number is 500 more than:

a 21 784 _____

b 10 645 _____

c 31 934 _____

d 15 814 _____

Activity 9

Use these digit cards to make:

a the highest 4-digit number _____

b the lowest 4-digit number _____

c the 4-digit number closest to 8000 _____

d the lowest 4-digit number between 5000 and 6000 _____

e Now make up six other numbers using these digits.

_____ _____ _____

_____ _____ _____

Activity 10

| 1 | 9 | 2 | 0 | 4 |

Use these digit cards to make:

a the highest 5-digit number _____

b the lowest 5-digit number _____

c the 5-digit number closest to 20 000 _____

d the lowest 5-digit number between
10 000 and 20 000 _____

Activity 11

Write these numbers in figures:

twenty-three thousand four hundred
and two _____

fourteen thousand six hundred and ten _____

fifty thousand and seven _____

nineteen thousand _____

Activity 12

Write these numbers in words:

10 456 _____

19 140 _____

18 203 _____

23 009 _____

2: Fractions

Activity 1

Shade half of each of these shapes.

Activity 2

Divide this rectangle into eighths and shade three of them.

What fraction is shaded? _____

What fraction is not shaded? _____

Activity 3

Divide this rectangle into tenths. Shade five of them.

What fraction is shaded? _____

Write this in another way. _____

What fraction is not shaded? _____

Write this in another way. _____

Activity 4

Find the fractions of the numbers.

a $\frac{1}{4}$ of 20 _____

b $\frac{3}{4}$ of 16 _____

c $\frac{1}{2}$ of 24 _____

d $\frac{1}{5}$ of 25 _____

e $\frac{2}{5}$ of 30 _____

f $\frac{4}{5}$ of 15 _____

g $\frac{1}{3}$ of 21 _____

h $\frac{1}{10}$ of 100 _____

Activity 5

Label the fraction strips with $\frac{1}{2}$, $\frac{1}{4}$ and $\frac{1}{8}$.

Use the fraction strips to find fractions that are equivalent to these:

$\frac{1}{2}$ _____ _____

$\frac{1}{4}$ _____

Activity 6

Fill in the missing fractions.

a $\frac{1}{2} + \boxed{} = 1$

b $\frac{1}{3} + \boxed{} = \frac{2}{3}$

c $\frac{1}{4} + \boxed{} = \frac{2}{4}$

d $\frac{2}{5} + \boxed{} = \frac{4}{5}$

e $\frac{3}{5} + \boxed{} = 1$

f $\frac{3}{6} + \boxed{} = \frac{5}{6}$

g $\frac{2}{7} + \boxed{} = \frac{5}{7}$

h $\frac{3}{10} + \boxed{} = \frac{9}{10}$

Activity 7

Order these fractions from smallest to largest.

$\frac{1}{5}$ $\frac{1}{3}$ $\frac{1}{2}$ $\frac{1}{10}$ $\frac{1}{4}$

0   1

Activity 8

Complete these equivalent fractions.

a $\frac{1}{2} = \frac{\square}{4}$

b $\frac{1}{4} = \frac{\square}{8}$

c $\frac{1}{3} = \frac{\square}{6}$

d $\frac{1}{5} = \frac{2}{\square}$

e $\frac{1}{2} = \frac{4}{\square}$

f $\frac{1}{6} = \frac{2}{\square}$

Activity 9

How many metres is:

$\frac{1}{2}$ of a kilometre? _____ $\frac{1}{10}$ of a kilometre? _____

$\frac{1}{4}$ of a kilometre? _____ $\frac{3}{10}$ of a kilometre? _____

$\frac{3}{4}$ of a kilometre? _____ $\frac{1}{5}$ of a kilometre? _____

$\frac{4}{5}$ of a kilometre? _____ $\frac{7}{10}$ of a kilometre? _____

You can use this number line to help you.

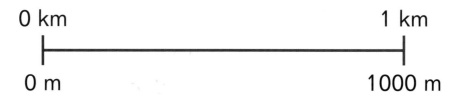

0 km   1 km

0 m   1000 m

Activity 10

How many minutes is:

$\frac{1}{2}$ of an hour? _____

$\frac{1}{4}$ of an hour? _____

$\frac{1}{3}$ of an hour? _____

$\frac{1}{6}$ of an hour? _____

$\frac{1}{12}$ of an hour? _____

$\frac{2}{3}$ of an hour? _____

$\frac{5}{6}$ of an hour? _____

$\frac{5}{12}$ of an hour? _____

You can use this clock to help you.

Activity 11

How many pence is:

$\frac{1}{2}$ of a £1? _____

$\frac{1}{4}$ of a £1? _____

$\frac{3}{4}$ of a £1? _____

$\frac{1}{5}$ of a £1? _____

$\frac{3}{5}$ of a £1? _____

$\frac{1}{10}$ of a £1? _____

$\frac{3}{10}$ of a £1? _____

$\frac{7}{10}$ of a £1? _____

You can use this number line to help you.

£0   £1

├─────────────────────────────────┤

0p   100p

3: Decimals

Activity 1

Plot the decimal numbers on the number line.

0.8   0.3   1.2   1.9   1.5   1.7

```
      ┌┬┬┬┬┬┬┬┬┬┬┬┬┬┬┬┬┬┬┬┐
      0              1              2
```

Activity 2

Order these decimals from smallest to largest.

23.2   14.5   29.8   17.9   20.1   19.3

_____

Activity 3

Round these decimals to the nearest whole number.

a   3.6 _____

b   4.2 _____

c   7.9 _____

d   12.1 _____

e   20.7 _____

f   21.5 _____

Activity 4

Write these lengths in two different ways.

Here is an example: 3 m 25 cm = 325 cm = 3.25 m

a   1 m 10 cm   _____   _____

b   2 m 5 cm   _____   _____

c   8 m 26 cm   _____   _____

d 10 m 15 cm _____ _____

e 15 m 75 cm _____ _____

f 20 m 50 cm _____ _____

Activity 5

Write these weights in two different ways.

Here is an example: 1 kg 250 g = 1 250 g = 1.25 kg

a 5 kg 300 g _____ _____

b 7 kg 125 g _____ _____

c 4 kg 275 g _____ _____

d 12 kg 500 g _____ _____

e 21 kg 175 g _____ _____

f 15 kg 325 g _____ _____

Activity 6

Write these capacities in two different ways.

Here is an example: 4 l 245 ml = 4 245 ml = 4.245 l

a 3 l 150 ml _____ _____

b 6 l 455 ml _____ _____

c 10 l 125 ml _____ _____

d 12 l 500 ml _____ _____

e 15 l 375 ml _____ _____

f 21 l 389 ml _____ _____

Activity 7

Write these amounts of money as pounds.

Here is an example: three pounds ten pence = £3.10

a six pounds thirty-five pence _____

b ten pounds sixty pence _____

c eight pounds twelve pence _____

d nineteen pounds five pence _____

e twenty-three pounds ninety-nine pence _____

f thirty pounds sixteen pence _____

Activity 8

Use the digits and the decimal place to make up as many different decimal numbers as you can.

Here are two examples: 46.9   6.49

Can you find another ten?

Write your decimals here:

Activity 9

Add these lengths:

a) 6.4 m + 5.7 m _____

b) 12.9 m + 10.6 m _____

c) 14.3 m + 9.8 m _____

Activity 10

Choose pairs of items to 'buy' from the list. Work out how much you will spend in total. Show how you worked out the total.

Trainers	£23.99
Jeans	£18.50
Jumper	£17.25
Jacket	£37.95

1st pair of items	2nd pair of items	3rd pair of items

Activity 11

Abbie had 6.5 m length of string. She cut off 2 m 75 cm and used it to tie up a package.

How much string did she have left?

_____

Activity 12

Alfie wants a laptop costing £348.99 and a printer costing £256.50. He has saved up £500. How much more does he need?

_____

4: Addition and subtraction

Activity 1

Add these two numbers together. **36   29**

Then find their difference.

Use a mental calculation strategy.

Show your strategy for addition here: Answer:	Show your strategy for subtraction here: Answer:

Activity 2

Add these numbers. Use a mental calculation strategy.

a 78 + 99

Show your strategy here:

b 36 + 37

Show your strategy here:

c 34 + 56

Show your strategy here:

Activity 3

Subtract these numbers. Use a mental calculation strategy.

a 100 − 76

Show your strategy here:

b 95 − 49

Show your strategy here:

c 86 − 79

Show your strategy here:

Activity 4

Make up some addition and subtraction calculations that have an answer of 40. Write your ideas around the circle. One has been done for you.

36 + 4 = 40

40

Activity 5

Choose two of these numbers to add together and then subtract. Then pick two more and do the same.

126   246   379

First pair of numbers: _____

Show how you added your numbers here: Answer:	Show how you subtracted your numbers here: Answer:

Second pair of numbers: _____

Show how you added your numbers here: Answer:	Show how you subtracted your numbers here: Answer:

Activity 6

Alfie had 58 stickers. Charlie had 29 more. How many stickers did Charlie have?

_____

Activity 7

Megan had 120 sweets. She gave 78 to Jamelia. How many did she have left?

_____

Activity 8

Amina baked 175 cakes for the cake sale. Alfie baked 212. They were hoping to sell 400. How many more cakes do they need to bake?

_____

Activity 9

Abbie had a collection of photographs. 134 of them were in one album, 248 were in another and 186 were in a third. How many photographs were in Abbie's collection?

_____

Activity 10

Kim had 126 stamps in her collection. Megan had twice as many as Kim. How many stamps did they have altogether?

_____

Activity 11

Abbie was aiming to score 175 points in the school quiz. She actually scored 133. How many more points did she need to get to reach 175?

_____

Activity 12

Charlie had 36 T-shirts, Alfie had 24, Amina had 26. How many T-shirts did they have altogether?

_____

5: Money

Activity 1

Find one of each of the coins that we use. Order them from least to greatest value.

Draw round each one in that order and label it.

Activity 2

In how many different ways can you make 50p?

List six of them here:

_____

_____

_____

_____

_____

Activity 3

In how many different ways can you make £1?

List eight of them here:

_____

_____

_____

_____

_____

Activity 4

Make £2.45 using the least number of coins.

Activity 5

Make £5.80 using the least number of coins.

Activity 6

Megan bought a doll. It cost £4.75. She paid the exact amount with 5 coins. Which coins did she use?

Coins that Megan used:

Activity 7

Amina bought a teddy bear. It cost £5.99. She handed in a £10 note and was given 3 coins in change. Which 3 coins was she given?

Coins that Amina was given:

Activity 8

Charlie bought a burger for £3.75 and a milkshake for £2.50. He paid the exact amount in coins. He used less than 10 coins. Which coins could he have paid with?

Coins that Charlie could have paid with:

Activity 9

Alfie, Jamelia and Abbie went
to a café for their lunch.

Price list	
Pizza per slice	£1.25
Salad bowl	£1.05
Ice cream	£0.90
Drink	£0.65

a Alfie bought 2 slices of pizza and a drink. How much did
he spend?

_____

b Jamelia bought 1 slice of pizza, a salad bowl and an ice
cream. How much did she spend?

_____

c Abbie bought 2 salad bowls, an ice cream and a drink.
How much did she spend?

_____

d What is their total bill?

_____

e They paid the total bill using the least number of coins
and notes. How did they pay? Draw the coins and
notes.

_____

Megan, Amina and Charlie bought some toys at their local toy shop.

Price list	
Remote control car	£25.95
Train set	£16.25
Football	£10.50
Robot	£15.65
Doll's pram	£23.18
Teddy bear	£9.98

a Megan bought 2 toys. She spent £39.43. Which toys did she buy?

_____

b Amina bought the car and teddy bear. How much did she spend?

_____

c Charlie bought a doll's pram, football and robot. How much change did he get from £50?

_____

d If you went to the shop and could choose 2 toys to buy, which would they be and how much would they cost you?

_____

6: Time

Activity 1

How many minutes are there in these?

Show your working.

a 1 hour _____

b $\frac{1}{2}$ hour _____

c $1\frac{1}{2}$ hours _____

d 2 hours _____

e 5 hours _____

f $\frac{3}{4}$ of an hour _____

Activity 2

How many seconds are there in these?

Show your working.

a 1 minute _____

b 2 minutes _____

c 5 minutes _____

d $2\frac{1}{2}$ minutes _____

e $\frac{3}{4}$ of a minute _____

f $3\frac{1}{2}$ minutes _____

Activity 3

How many hours are there in these?

Show your working.

a 1 day _____

b 2 days _____

c 5 days   _____

d 10 days   _____

e 7 days   _____

Activity 4

How many days are there in these?

Show your working.

a 1 week   _____

b 2 weeks   _____

c 10 weeks   _____

d 12 weeks   _____

e 20 weeks   _____

Activity 5

Circle the words that are used to describe time:

hours   capacity   later   heavy   light   early

millennium   century   contains   metres

Activity 6

Abbie left home at 7.00 a.m. and returned at 10.45 a.m. How long was she away?

You might find it helpful to use a time number line:

7.00   11.30

Activity 7

Use time number lines to find the following time differences:

10.15 a.m. to 12.30 p.m.

Draw your time number line here:

9.45 a.m. to 1.15 p.m.

Draw your time number line here:

9.30 a.m. to 2.45 p.m.

Draw your time number line here:

Activity 8

Draw the times on these clocks and label them with the digital times. Don't forget to put a.m. or p.m.!

a Quarter past 7 (morning) **b** 20 to 3 (afternoon) **c** 25 past 12 (afternoon)

Digital time:

Digital time:

Digital time:

7: Measures – length

Circle the words that show the units we use to measure length.

millimetres   millilitres   kilograms   metres
kilometres   grams   litres   miles   feet

Activity 2

Write the abbreviations for these measures of length.

a centimetres _____   **c** kilometres _____

b millimetres _____   **d** metres _____

Activity 3

Circle the words that are connected with length.

width   heavy   height   contains   long   short
light   empty   full   tall

Activity 4

Write these millimetre lengths in two different ways.

Here is an example: 22 mm = 2 cm 2 mm = 2.2 cm

a 45 mm _____   **c** 14 mm _____

b 36 mm _____   **d** 64 mm _____

Activity 5

Write these centimetre lengths in two different ways.

Here is an example: 132 cm = 1 m 32 cm = 1.32 m

a 245 cm _____   **c** 209 cm _____

b 360 cm _____   **d** 340 cm _____

Write these metre lengths in two different ways.

Here is an example: 2200 m = 2 km 200 m = 2.2 km

a 4500 m _____   **d** 1050 m _____

b 1536 m _____   **e** 6600 m _____

c 2090 m _____

Activity 7

Alfie, Megan and Abbie had lengths of string. Alfie had a length of 10 cm 5 mm, Megan had a length twice as long as Alfie's and Abbie had one that totalled the length of Alfie's and Megan's.

How long were Megan's and Abbie's lengths of string?

Megan: _____   Abbie: _____

Activity 8

Kim went for a run. She ran at 6.5 km per hour. She ran for $1\frac{1}{2}$ hours.

How far did she run in metres?

Distance: _____

8: Measures – mass

Activity 1

Circle the words that show the units we use to measure mass.

centimetres litres grams metres kilometres kilograms
millilitres pounds ounces

Activity 2

Write the abbreviations for these measures of mass.

a grams _____ **b** kilograms _____

Activity 3

Circle the words that are connected with mass.

weigh heavy height long light empty full height

Activity 4

Circle the names of the equipment we use to measure mass.

weighing scales cylinder measuring jug ruler balance

Activity 5

Write these gram masses in two different ways.

Here is an example: 1522 g = 1 kg 522 g = 1.522 kg

a 1750 g _____   **d** 5500 g _____

b 3600 g _____   **e** 1575 g _____

c 1290 g _____   **f** 1675 g _____

Activity 6

Order these masses from lightest to heaviest.

500 g 1.2 kg 750 g 0.4 kg 1 kg 100 g 1300 g 1.25 kg

_____

29

Activity 7

Kim, Amina and Charlie weighed the pebbles they had collected at the beach. The mass of Kim's was twice as much as Charlie's and half the mass of Amina's. Amina had 3 kg of pebbles. What were the masses of Kim's and Charlie's pebbles?

Kim: Charlie:
_____

What was the total mass of the pebbles collected by Kim, Amina and Charlie?

Mass: _____

Activity 8

Alfie weighs 48.5 kg. Jamelia weighs 46.25 kg. How much heavier than Jamelia is Alfie?

_____

What is their total mass?

_____

9: Measures – capacity

Activity 1

Circle the words that show the units we use to measure capacity:

grams   centimetres   litres   metres   kilometres   gallons   kilograms   millilitres   pints

Activity 2

Write the abbreviations for these measures of capacity.

a litres _____   **b** millilitres _____

Activity 3

Circle the words that are connected with capacity.

liquid   heavy   empty   long   light   width   full   height

Activity 4

Circle the names of the equipment we use to measure capacity.

cylinder   metre stick   measuring jug   ruler   balance

Activity 5

Write these millilitre capacities in two different ways.

Here is an example: 2500 ml = 2 l 500 ml = 2.5 l

a 1500 ml _____

b 3750 ml _____

c 5750 ml _____

d 4500 ml _____

e 2775 ml _____

f 3225 ml _____

Activity 6

Order these capacities from least to most:

500 ml   1.4 l   725 ml   0.8 l   2 l 250 ml   1200 ml   1.35 l

Activity 7

Kim, Abbie and Charlie each filled their water pistols with water. Kim's pistol held twice as much as Charlie's and three times the amount of Abbie's. Abbie's held 1.5 l of water.

What were the capacities of Kim's and Charlie's water pistols?

Kim: _____   Charlie: _____

What was the total capacity of Kim's, Abbie's and Charlie's water pistols?

Capacity: _____

Activity 8

Alfie needs 250 ml of concentrate to make 1 litre of squash. He wants to make 5 litres of squash. How much concentrate does he need?

10: Puzzles

Activity 1

1 If you add 25 to a number, you get 68. What is the number? _____

2 If you take 13 away from a number, you get 49. What is the number? _____

3 If you halve a number and add 10, you get 36. What is the number? _____

4 If you double a number and take away 20, you get 50. What is the number? _____

Activity 2

Write down all the factors of 24. _____

Activity 3

Circle the numbers that are factors of 40.

5   12   8   20   15   10   1   40   2

Activity 4

Write down eight multiples of 3. _____

Activity 5

Circle the numbers that are multiples of 6.

5   10   12   15   20   24   30   35   42   48

Activity 6

Circle the numbers that are multiples of both 3 and 9.

6   12   18   24   27   32   36   45   49   54

Activity 7

Write these numbers in the correct parts of this Venn diagram:

12 15 20 21
24 25 27 31
40 45 48 49
50

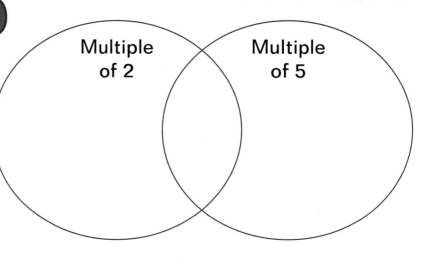

Multiple of 2

Multiple of 5

What do you notice about the numbers in the overlap of the two circles?

Activity 8

Put at least five numbers in each section of the Carroll diagram.

	Multiples of 3	Not multiples of 3
Even		
Not even		

Activity 9

Circle the square numbers.

12   16   21   25   30   36   40   49   54   64

Activity 10

Put the right signs in these number sentences to make them correct. Use addition and subtraction.

a   84 ☐ 12 ☐ 16 = 80

b   35 ☐ 29 ☐ 32 = 38

c   82 ☐ 23 ☐ 58 = 1

11: Patterns and sequences

Activity 1

Write the next three numbers in these number sequences.

a   4   8   12   16   ☐ ☐ ☐

b   35   30   25   20   ☐ ☐ ☐

c   14   21   28   35   ☐ ☐ ☐

d   81   72   63   54   ☐ ☐ ☐

e   30   36   42   48   ☐ ☐ ☐

f   2   4   8   16   ☐ ☐ ☐

Activity 2

Complete these number sequences.

a   100   ☐   70   ☐   40   ☐   10

b   12   ☐   36   ☐   60   ☐   84

c   ☐   ☐   25   ☐   35   40   ☐

d   ☐   16   ☐   ☐   40   48   56

e   77   ☐   ☐   44   33   ☐   ☐

f   150   125   ☐   ☐   50   ☐   ☐

Activity 3

Fill the missing numbers in these parts of a 100 square.

	26	
35	36	

	78	
87		

		90
	99	

21		23	
31			

18	
37	

74	
85	

Activity 4

Shade all the multiples of 2 in one colour. Shade all the multiples of 3 in another.

1	2	3	4	5	6	7	8	9	10
11	12	13	14	15	16	17	18	19	20
21	22	23	24	25	26	27	28	29	30
31	32	33	34	35	36	37	38	39	40
41	42	43	44	45	46	47	48	49	50
51	52	53	54	55	56	57	58	59	60
61	62	63	64	65	66	67	68	69	70
71	72	73	74	75	76	77	78	79	80
81	82	83	84	85	86	87	88	89	90
91	92	93	94	95	96	97	98	99	100

Write the numbers that are multiples of both 2 and 3.

Activity 5

Shade the 100 square to complete the pattern.

1	2	3	4	5	6	7	8	9	10
11	12	13	14	15	16	17	18	19	20
21	22	23	24	25	26	27	28	29	30
31	32	33	34	35	36	37	38	39	40
41	42	43	44	45	46	47	48	49	50
51	52	53	54	55	56	57	58	59	60
61	62	63	64	65	66	67	68	69	70
71	72	73	74	75	76	77	78	79	80
81	82	83	84	85	86	87	88	89	90
91	92	93	94	95	96	97	98	99	100

Activity 6

Make up some number sequences with these starting numbers. For each write your rule.

a 3 | | | | | | | | | |

My rule: _____

b 5 | | | | | | | | | |

My rule: _____

c 12 | | | | | | | | | |

My rule: _____

d 20 | | | | | | | | | |

My rule: _____

Activity 7

Make up some number sequences with these finishing numbers. For each write your rule.

a | | | | | | | | | | 100

My rule: _____

b | | | | | | | | | | 50

My rule: _____

c | | | | | | | | | | 28

My rule: _____

d | | | | | | | | | | 125

My rule: _____

12: Multiplication and division

Activity 1

Look at this array of dots.

○○○○○○○○ Write two multiplication and division
○○○○○○○○ sentences to describe the array.
○○○○○○○○
○○○○○○○○

Two multiplication sentences:

_____

Two division sentences:

_____

How many dots are there altogether? _____

Activity 2

Draw an array of dots to show $6 \times 3 = 18$.

Activity 3

Answer these multiplications.

a 4×5 _____   **f** 9×6 _____

b 6×4 _____   **g** 5×9 _____

c 8×3 _____   **h** 4×8 _____

d 7×8 _____   **i** 6×3 _____

e 8×5 _____   **j** 7×4 _____

Activity 4

Make up two multiplication sentences and two division sentences using these numbers:

a   4   6   24 _____

_____

b   36   4   9 _____

_____

c   70   10   7 _____

_____

d   6   8   48 _____

_____

e   3   7   21 _____

_____

f   54   6   9 _____

_____

g   4   9   36 _____

_____

h   5   8   40 _____

_____

i   42   7   6 _____

_____

j   56   8   7 _____

_____

Activity 5

Solve these divisions.

a 28 ÷ 7 _____

b 24 ÷ 6 _____

c 36 ÷ 9 _____

d 72 ÷ 8 _____

e 45 ÷ 5 _____

f 48 ÷ 6 _____

g 27 ÷ 9 _____

h 42 ÷ 7 _____

i 70 ÷ 10 _____

j 63 ÷ 7 _____

Activity 6

Square all the numbers up to and including 10.

1 × 1 = ___

2 × 2 = ___

3 × 3 = ___

4 × 4 = ___

5 × 5 = ___

6 × 6 = ___

7 × 7 = ___

8 × 8 = ___

9 × 9 = ___

10 × 10 = ___

Activity 7

Write down these tables from 1× to 12×.

6× table	7× table

Activity 8

Answer these:

a 125 × 6

Show your method:

b 234 × 5

Show your method:

c 245 × 4

Show your method:

Activity 9

Kim bought three boxes. In each box there were 24 doughnuts. How many doughnuts did she have altogether?

Show your method:

Activity 10

Charlie stuck his football stickers onto a large piece of paper. He made them into an array which had 6 columns and 58 rows. How many stickers did he have?

Show your method:

13: 2D shapes

Activity 1

Label these shapes with their names.

_____ _____ _____ _____

_____ _____ _____ _____

Activity 2

Draw all the lines of symmetry on this square.

Activity 3

Draw all the lines of symmetry on this rectangle.

Activity 4

Draw a triangle with three lines of symmetry. Show the lines of symmetry.

Activity 5

Draw a triangle with one line of symmetry. Show the line of symmetry.

Activity 6

Draw 2D shapes in the Carroll diagram.

	Right angles	Not right angles
4 sides		
Not 4 sides		

Activity 7

Draw three different triangles. Label them with these labels: isosceles, equilateral and scalene.

Activity 8

Draw four different quadrilaterals. Can you name them?

Activity 9

How many rectangles can you see? There are more than 9!

14: 3D shapes

Activity 1

Label these shapes with their names and properties.

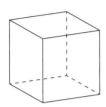

Name: _____

Number of faces: _____

Number of edges: _____

Number of vertices: _____

Shape of faces: _____

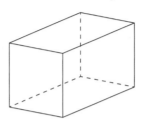

Name: _____

Number of faces: _____

Number of edges: _____

Number of vertices: _____

Shape of faces: _____

Name: _____

Number of faces: _____

Number of edges: _____

Number of vertices: _____

Shape of faces: _____

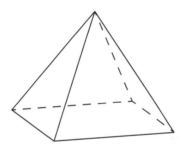

Name: _____

Number of faces: _____

Number of edges: _____

Number of vertices: _____

Shape of faces: _____

Activity 2

Think of a 3D shape to go into each section of this Carroll diagram.

	Square faces	Not square faces
Prism		
Not prism		

Activity 3

Use the clues to identify the shapes:

a 6 square faces   _____

b 5 faces, one is a square _____

c 9 edges, prism   _____

d 8 vertices, rectangular face _____

e 4 triangular faces   _____

Activity 4

Imagine a square-based pyramid. Draw its net.

Test it out on paper. Does it work?

Activity 5

Imagine a cube. Draw its net.

Test it out on paper. Does it work?

Activity 6

Now draw and test another net for a cube.

15: Position and direction

● **Activity 1**

Label the 8 compass points on this compass.

● **Activity 2**

1 If you are facing north and make a $\frac{3}{4}$ clockwise turn, where will you be facing?

_____

2 If you are facing south and make a $\frac{1}{4}$ anticlockwise turn, where will you be facing?

_____

3 If you face east and make an anticlockwise turn through 2 right angles, where will you be facing?

_____

4 If you face west and make a clockwise turn through 1 right angle, where will you be facing?

_____

5 If you face south-east and make a $\frac{1}{4}$ clockwise turn, where will you be facing?

_____

6 If you face north-west and make a $\frac{3}{4}$ anticlockwise turn, where will you be facing?

_____

7 If you face south-west and make a $\frac{1}{4}$ clockwise turn, where will you be facing?

_____

Activity 3

Turn the arrow so that it faces south. Draw it in its new position.

What turn did you make and in which direction?

N

↑

_____

_____

Can you turn it in another direction
to put it in this position?

_____

Activity 4

Turn the arrow so that it faces north. Draw it in its new position.

What turn did you make and in which direction?

→

_____

_____

Can you turn it in another direction
to put it in this position?

_____

Activity 5

Turn the arrow so that it faces south. Draw it in its new position.

What turn did you make and in which direction?

←

_____

_____

Can you turn it in another direction
to put it in this position?

_____

Activity 6

In which direction are the arrows facing? The top of the page is north.

a _____

b _____

c _____

d _____

e _____

f _____

g _____

Activity 7

Use compass directions to describe the routes.

a Describe the route you can take from the hut to the lighthouse.

_____

_____

_____

b Describe the route you can take from the volcano to the mountain.

_____

_____

_____

c Describe the route the dolphin could take to the small island.

_____

_____

_____

Activity 8

Use the map to make up your own route from one place to another.

Describe it below.

_____

_____

_____

_____

Activity 9

In which compass directions are these:

a The volcano from the mountain? _____

b The lighthouse from the hut? _____

c The cave from the cat? _____

d The dolphin from the volcano? _____

e The ship from the lighthouse? _____

f The cat from the mountain? _____

g The mouse from the lighthouse? _____

h The lighthouse from the volcano? _____

i The cave from the mountain? _____

16: Data handling

Activity 1

This bar graph shows the number of pets sold in a pet shop over one month.

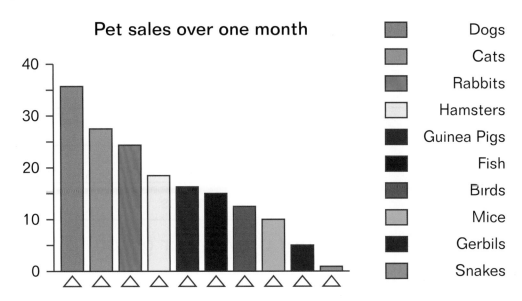

Pet sales over one month

■	Dogs
■	Cats
■	Rabbits
☐	Hamsters
■	Guinea Pigs
■	Fish
■	Birds
☐	Mice
■	Gerbils
■	Snakes

Use the graph to estimate the answers to these questions.

a How many of each pet were bought?

dogs	_____	cats	_____
guinea pigs	_____	fish	_____
birds	_____	mice	_____
gerbils	_____	snakes	_____
rabbits	_____	hamsters	_____

b What is the total number of pets sold? _____

c How many more dogs were bought than rabbits? _____

d How many more cats were sold than mice? _____

e At this shop which are the four most popular pets? _____

This table shows the number of sales at another pet shop.

Pets	Number	Pets	Number
Dogs	42	Fish	5
Cats	36	Birds	9
Rabbits	14	Mice	3
Hamsters	17	Gerbils	12
Guinea Pigs	20	Snakes	5

On a separate piece of paper draw a bar graph to show this information.

a What is the difference in the sales of gerbils in the two pet shops? _____

b What is the difference in the sales of dogs in the two pet shops? _____

c What is the difference in the sales of snakes in the two pet shops? _____

d What is the total number of rabbits sold in the two pet shops? _____

e What is the total number of birds sold in the two pet shops? _____

f Which pet shop sold the most pets during the month? _____

Use this space to work out your answer.

Activity 3

Draw a pictogram to show the information in the table.

Choose your own symbol.

Each symbol needs to represent two people.

Favourite colour	Number of people
Red	20
Blue	34
Black	10
Purple	15
Yellow	21
Orange	12
White	8

a Make up three statements from your pictogram:

_____

_____

_____

b Which are the three most popular colours?

_____

c Which are the three least popular colours?

_____

Activity 4

Answer the questions from the bar graph below:

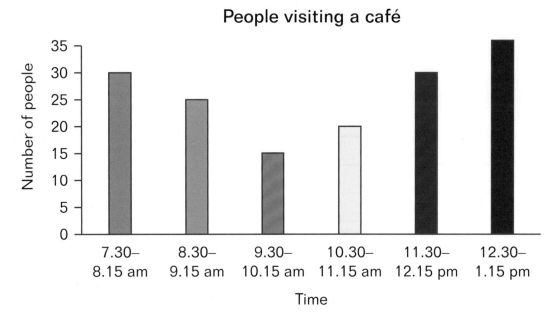

People visiting a café

a Which is the busiest time of the day?

_____

b Which is the least busy time of the day?

_____

c How many people visited the café between 8.30 and 9.15 a.m.?

_____

d How many more people visited the café between 7.30 and 8.15 a.m. than during the least busy time?

_____

e How many people were in the café at 10.00 a.m.?

_____

f What was the total number of people visiting the café?

_____

17: Two-step problems

Activity 1

Jamelia had saved £25. She spent £6.99 on a book and £8.50 on a CD. How much money did she have left?

_____

Activity 2

Kim bought 3 packets of biscuits at £2.25 each. How much change did she get from £10?

_____

Activity 3

Charlie bought 36 toy cars. $\frac{1}{2}$ of them were red, $\frac{1}{3}$ of those left were blue and the rest were black. How many were black?

_____

Activity 4

Amina had a packet of biscuits. There were 24 in the packet. $\frac{1}{4}$ of them were chocolate, $\frac{1}{3}$ were shortbread and the rest were ginger. How many ginger biscuits were there?

_____

Activity 5

There were 100 people at the football match. $\frac{1}{2}$ of them were grown-ups, the rest were children. $\frac{2}{5}$ of the children were girls. How many boys were at the match?

_____

Activity 6

There were 136 plastic cups in a carton. Kim had 3 cartons. She used 350 plastic cups to serve drinks at the school disco. How many cups were left?

_____

Activity 7

A crate of 248 books arrived at the library. Mrs Smith wanted to put $\frac{1}{2}$ of them in equal numbers on 4 shelves. How many books were on each shelf?

_____

Activity 8

There were 32 children in each class at Fire Tree Lane Junior School and four year groups. Each year group had 2 classes. How many children were at the school?

_____

Activity 9

In each of their matches the netball team scored 4 goals. They played 2 matches each week for 12 weeks. How many goals did they score altogether?

_____

Activity 10

Megan bought 3 boxes of chocolates at £3.50 each and 2 boxes costing £4.75 each. How much did Megan spend on chocolates?

_____

Activity 11

Alfie made 24 jugs of juice. Each jug needed 50 ml of juice concentrate. How much concentrate did he use in total?

_____

Activity 12

Jamelia ordered 4 boxes of pencils. Each box had 10 pencils. The order cost Jamelia £10.40. How much is one pencil?

_____

Activity 13

Alfie, Amina and Jamelia each buy a sandwich for £3.65 and a drink for £2.20. How much do they spend altogether?

_____

Activity 14

The school ordered sports equipment. They ordered 4 footballs, each costing £12.50 and 2 five-a-side goal posts, each costing £47.99. How much did they spend altogether?

_____

Activity 15

Charlie bought 6 packets of party poppers to give to his friends at his birthday party. The party poppers cost £3.56 per pack. There was a 'buy one and get one for half price' offer.

He used the offer. How much did he spend on party poppers?

_____

Answers

Unit 1

1 Close estimates are acceptable.

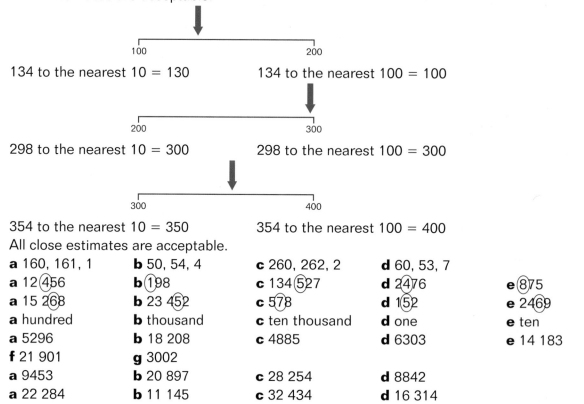

134 to the nearest 10 = 130   134 to the nearest 100 = 100

298 to the nearest 10 = 300   298 to the nearest 100 = 300

354 to the nearest 10 = 350   354 to the nearest 100 = 400

2 All close estimates are acceptable.

    a 160, 161, 1   **b** 50, 54, 4   **c** 260, 262, 2   **d** 60, 53, 7

3 **a** 12 4̲5̲6   **b** 1̲98   **c** 134 5̲27   **d** 24̲76   **e** 8̲75

4 **a** 15 2̲68   **b** 23 4̲52   **c** 5̲78   **d** 15̲2   **e** 246̲9

5 **a** hundred   **b** thousand   **c** ten thousand   **d** one   **e** ten

6 **a** 5296   **b** 18 208   **c** 4885   **d** 6303   **e** 14 183

    f 21 901   **g** 3002

7 **a** 9453   **b** 20 897   **c** 28 254   **d** 8842

8 **a** 22 284   **b** 11 145   **c** 32 434   **d** 16 314

9 **a** 8765   **b** 5678   **c** 7865   **d** 5678   **e** Children's choices

10 **a** 94 210   **b** 10 249   **c** 20 149   **d** 10 249

11 23 402, 14 610, 50 007, 19 000

12 ten thousand four hundred and fifty-six
nineteen thousand one hundred and forty
eighteen thousand two hundred and three
twenty-three thousand and nine

Unit 2

1 Any answer where the shapes have been divided into two equal parts

2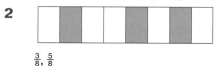

$\frac{3}{8}, \frac{5}{8}$

3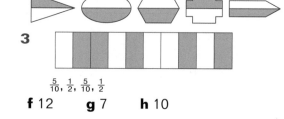

$\frac{5}{10}, \frac{1}{2}, \frac{5}{10}, \frac{1}{2}$

4 **a** 5   **b** 12   **c** 12   **d** 5   **e** 12   **f** 12   **g** 7   **h** 10

5

	$\frac{1}{2}$		$\frac{1}{2}$	
$\frac{1}{4}$		$\frac{1}{4}$	$\frac{1}{4}$	$\frac{1}{4}$
$\frac{1}{8}$	$\frac{1}{8}$	$\frac{1}{8}$ $\frac{1}{8}$	$\frac{1}{8}$ $\frac{1}{8}$	$\frac{1}{8}$ $\frac{1}{8}$

$\frac{2}{4}, \frac{4}{8}, \frac{2}{8}$

6 **a** $\frac{1}{2}$ **b** $\frac{1}{3}$ **c** $\frac{1}{4}$ **d** $\frac{2}{5}$ **e** $\frac{2}{5}$ **f** $\frac{2}{6}$ **g** $\frac{3}{7}$ **h** $\frac{6}{10}$

7 $\frac{1}{10}, \frac{1}{5}, \frac{1}{4}, \frac{1}{3}, \frac{1}{2}$ **8** **a** $\frac{2}{4}$ **b** $\frac{2}{8}$ **c** $\frac{2}{6}$ **d** $\frac{2}{10}$ **e** $\frac{4}{8}$ **f** $\frac{2}{12}$

9 500 m, 250 m, 750 m, 800 m, 100 m, 300 m, 200 m, 700 m

10 30 minutes, 15 minutes, 20 minutes, 10 minutes, 5 minutes, 40 minutes, 50 minutes, 25 minutes

11 50p, 25p, 75p, 20p, 60p, 10p, 30p, 70p

Unit 3

1

2   14.5, 17.9, 19.3, 20.1, 23.2, 29.8

3   **a** 4 **b** 4 **c** 8 **d** 12 **e** 21 **f** 22

4   **a** 110 cm, 1.1 m **b** 205 cm, 2.05 m **c** 826 cm, 8.26 m
    d 1015 cm, 10.15 m **e** 1575 cm, 15.75 m **f** 2050 cm, 20.5 m

5   **a** 5300 g, 5.3 kg **b** 7125 g, 7.125 kg **c** 4275 g, 4.275 kg
    d 12 500 g, 12.5 kg **e** 21 175 g, 21.175 kg **f** 15 325 g, 15.325 kg

6   **a** 3150 ml, 3.15 l **b** 6455 ml, 6.455 l **c** 10 125 ml, 10.125 l
    d 12 500 ml, 12.5 l **e** 15 375 ml, 15.375 l **f** 21 389 ml, 21.389 l

7   **a** £6.35 **b** £10.60 **c** £8.12 **d** £19.05 **e** £23.99 **f** £30.16

8   64.9, 49.6, 94.6, 69.4, 96.4, 6.94, 4.69, 4.96, 9.64, 9.46

9   **a** 12.1 m **b** 23.5 m **c** 24.1 m

10 Answers depend on the children's choices.

11 3.75 m or 3 m 75 cm

12 £105.49

Unit 4

1   65, 7   2   **a** 177 **b** 73 **c** 90   3   **a** 24 **b** 46 **c** 7

4   All number sentences need to have the answer of 40.

5   Answers depend on children's choices of numbers.

6   87   7   42   8   13   9   568

10 378   11   42   12   86

Unit 5

1   Pictures of all coins in order from 1p to £2

2   There are many ways to make 50p. Examples: 1 × 50p, 5 × 10p, 10 × 5p, 25 × 2p,
    50 × 1p, 2 × 20p + 10p, 1 × 20p + 3 × 10p

3   There are many ways to make £1. Examples: 1 × £1, 2 × 50p, 5 × 20p, 10 × 10p,
    20 × 5p, 1 × 50p + 2 × 20p + 1 × 10p, 1 × 50p + 5 × 10p, 1 × 50p + 10 × 5p

4   1 × £2, 2 × 20p, 1 × 5p

5   2 × £2, 1 × £1, 1 × 50p, 1 × 20p, 1 × 10p

6   2 × £2, 1 × 50p, 1 × 20p, 1 × 5p

7   2 × £2, 1 × 1p

8   Example answer: 3 × £2, 1 × 20p, 1 × 5p

9   **a** £3.15 **b** £3.20 **c** £3.65 **d** £10 **e** 1 × £10

10 **a** train set, **b** £35.93 **c** £0.67 **d** Answer depends on
    doll's pram   children's choices

Unit 6

1   **a** 60 minutes **b** 30 minutes **c** 90 minutes **d** 120 minutes **e** 300 minutes **f** 45 minutes

2   **a** 60 seconds **b** 120 seconds **c** 300 seconds **d** 150 seconds **e** 45 seconds **f** 210 seconds

3   **a** 24 hours **b** 48 hours **c** 120 hours **d** 240 hours **e** 168 hours

4   **a** 7 days **b** 14 days **c** 70 days **d** 84 days **e** 140 days

5   (hours)   capacity   (later)   heavy   light   (early)   (millennium)   (century)
    contains   metres

6   3 hours 45 minutes

7 2 hours 15 minutes, $3\frac{1}{2}$ hours, 5 hours 15 minutes

8

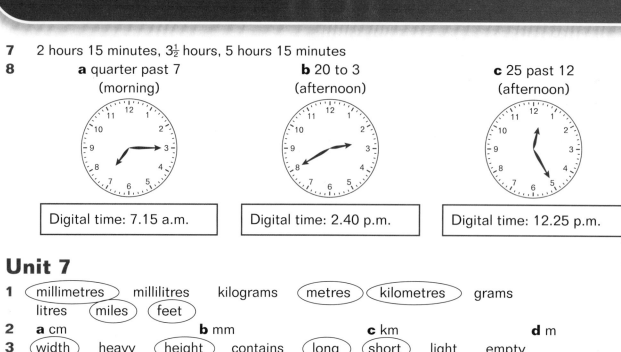

a quarter past 7 (morning)   Digital time: 7.15 a.m.

b 20 to 3 (afternoon)   Digital time: 2.40 p.m.

c 25 past 12 (afternoon)   Digital time: 12.25 p.m.

Unit 7

1 (millimetres) millilitres kilograms (metres) (kilometres) grams litres (miles) (feet)

2 **a** cm   **b** mm   **c** km   **d** m

3 (width) heavy (height) contains (long) (short) light empty full (tall)

4 **a** 4 cm 5 mm = 4.5 cm   **b** 3 cm 6 mm = 3.6 cm   **c** 1 cm 4 mm = 1.4 cm
   d 6 cm 4 mm = 6.4 cm

5 **a** 2 m 45 cm = 2.45 m   **b** 3 m 60 cm = 3.6 m   **c** 2 m 9 cm = 2.09 m
   d 3 m 40 cm = 3.4 m

6 **a** 4 km 500 m = 4.5 km   **b** 1 km 536 m = 1.536 km   **c** 2 km 90 m = 2.09 km
   d 1 km 50 m = 1.05 km   **e** 6 km 600 m = 6.6 km

7 Megan: 21 cm, Abbie: 31.5 cm (31 cm 5 mm)

8 9750 m

Unit 8

1 centimetres litres (grams) metres kilometres (kilograms) millilitres (pounds) (ounces)

2 **a** g   **b** kg

3 (weigh) (heavy) height long (light) empty full height

4 (weighing scales) cylinder measuring jug ruler (balance)

5 **a** 1 kg 750 g = 1.75 kg   **b** 3 kg 600 g = 3.6 kg   **c** 1 kg 290 g = 1.29 kg
   d 5 kg 500 g = 5.5 kg   **e** 1 kg 575 g = 1.575 kg   **f** 1 kg 675 g = 1.675 kg

6 0.4 kg, 500 g, 750 g, 1 kg 100 g, 1.2 kg, 1.25 kg, 1300 g

7 Kim's 1.5 kg, Charlie's 750 g   Total: 5.25 kg or 5 kg 250 g

8 2.25 kg or 2 kg 250 g   Total: 94.75 kg or 94 kg 750 g

Unit 9

1 grams centimetres (litres) metres kilometres (gallons) kilograms (millilitres) (pints)

2 **a** l   **b** ml

3 (liquid) heavy (empty) long light width (full) height

4 (cylinder) metre stick (measuring jug) ruler balance

5 **a** 1 l 500 ml = 1.5 l   **b** 3 l 750 ml = 3.75 l   **c** 5 l 750 ml = 5.75 l   **d** 4 l 500 ml = 4.5 l
   e 2 l 775 ml = 2.775 l   **f** 3 l 225 ml = 3.225 l

6 500 ml, 725 ml, 0.8 l, 1200 ml, 1.35 l, 1.4 l, 2 l 250 ml

7 Kim: 4.5 l, Charlie: 2.25 l   Total: 8.25 l or 8 l 250 ml

8 1 l 250 ml or 1.25 l

Unit 10

1 **1** 43 **2** 62 **3** 52 **4** 35

2 1, 2, 3, 4, 6, 8, 12, 24

3 (5) 12 (8) (20) 15 (10) (1) (40) (2)

4 No fixed answer. Examples could include anything in the 3× table.

5 5 10 (12) 15 20 (24) (30) 35 (42) (48)

6 6 12 (18) 24 (27) 32 (36) (45) 49 (54)

7

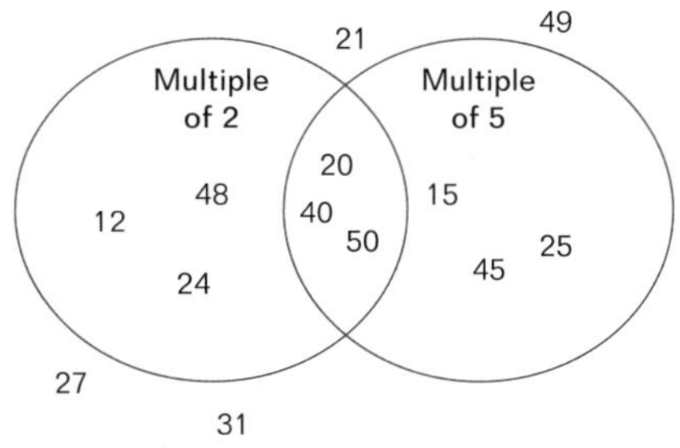

20, 40 and 50 are multiples of 2 and 5

8 Answers depend on the children's choices. Example:

	Multiples of 3	Not multiples of 3
Even	6, 12, 18, 24	8, 14, 22, 34
Not even	9, 15, 21, 27	1, 5, 13, 25

9 12 (16) 21 (25) 30 (36) 40 (49) 54 (64)

10 **a** 84 [+] 12 [−] 16 = 80 **b** 35 [−] 29 [+] 32 = 38 **c** 82 [−] 23 [−] 58 = 1

Unit 11

1 **a** 20, 24, 28 **b** 15, 10, 5 **c** 42, 49, 56 **d** 45, 36, 27 **e** 54, 60, 66 **f** 32, 64, 128

2 **a** 100, 85, 70, 55, 40, 25, 10 **b** 12, 24, 36, 48, 60, 72, 84 **c** 15, 20, 25, 30, 35, 40, 45
d 8, 16, 24, 32, 40, 48, 56 **e** 77, 66, 55, 44, 33, 22, 11 **f** 150, 125, 100, 75, 50, 25, 0

3

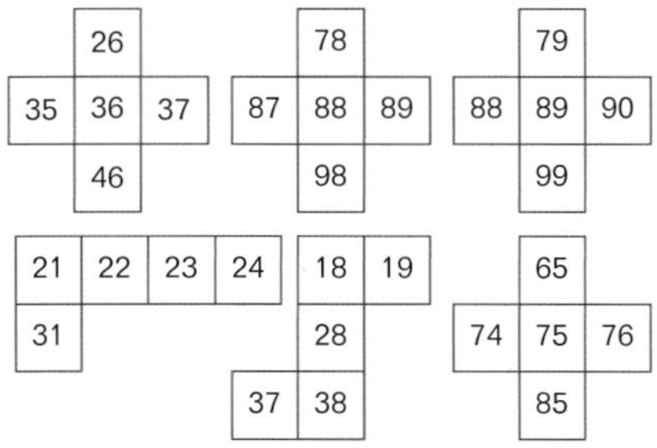

4

1	2	3	4	5	6	7	8	9	10
11	12	13	14	15	16	17	18	19	20
21	22	23	24	25	26	27	28	29	30
31	32	33	34	35	36	37	38	39	40
41	42	43	44	45	46	47	48	49	50
51	52	53	54	55	56	57	58	59	60
61	62	63	64	65	66	67	68	69	70
71	72	73	74	75	76	77	78	79	80
81	82	83	84	85	86	87	88	89	90
91	92	93	94	95	96	97	98	99	100

Multiples of both 2 and 3: 6, 12, 18, 24, 30, 36, 42, 48, 54, 60, 66, 72, 78, 84, 90, 96

5

1	**2**	3	4	**5**	6	7	8	**9**	10
11	12	13	**14**	15	16	17	18	19	**20**
21	22	23	24	25	26	**27**	28	29	30
31	32	33	34	**35**	36	37	38	39	40
41	42	43	**44**	45	46	47	48	49	50
51	52	53	**54**	55	56	57	58	59	60
61	62	63	64	**65**	66	67	68	69	70
71	72	73	74	75	76	**77**	78	79	80
81	82	83	84	85	86	87	88	89	**90**
91	92	93	94	95	96	97	98	99	100

6   Answers depend on the children's choices.

7   Answers depend on the children's choices.

Unit 12

1   8 × 4 = 32, 4 × 8 = 32, 32 ÷ 4 = 8, 32 ÷ 8 = 4, 32

2   ○○○○○○
○○○○○○
○○○○○○

3   **a** 20   **b** 24   **c** 24   **d** 56   **e** 40   **f** 54   **g** 45   **h** 32   **i** 18   **j** 28

4   **a** 6 × 4 = 24, 4 × 6 = 24, 24 ÷ 6 = 4, 24 ÷ 4 = 6
  b 4 × 9 = 36, 9 × 4 = 36, 36 ÷ 4 = 9, 36 ÷ 9 = 4
  c 10 × 7 = 70, 7 × 10 = 70, 70 ÷ 7 = 10, 70 ÷ 10 = 7
  d 6 × 8 = 48, 8 × 6 = 48, 48 ÷ 6 = 8, 48 ÷ 8 = 6
  e 3 × 7 = 21, 7 × 3 = 21, 21 ÷ 3 = 7, 21 ÷ 7 = 3
  f 6 × 9 = 54, 9 × 6 = 54, 54 ÷ 6 = 9, 54 ÷ 9 = 6
  g 4 × 9 = 36, 9 × 4 = 36, 36 ÷ 9 = 4, 36 ÷ 4 = 9
  h 5 × 8 = 40, 8 × 5 = 40, 40 ÷ 8 = 5, 40 ÷ 5 = 8
  i 6 × 7 = 42, 7 × 6 = 42, 42 ÷ 6 = 7, 42 ÷ 7 = 6
  j 7 × 8 = 56, 8 × 7 = 56, 56 ÷ 7 = 8, 56 ÷ 8 = 7

5   **a** 4   **b** 4   **c** 4   **d** 9   **e** 9   **f** 8   **g** 3   **h** 6   **i** 7   **j** 9

6   1, 4, 9, 16, 25, 36, 49, 64, 81, 100

7   6, 12, 18, 24, 30, 36, 42, 48, 54, 60, 66, 72
   7, 14, 21, 28, 35, 42, 49, 56, 63, 70, 77, 84

8   **a** 750 **b** 1170 **c** 980   **9**   72   **10**   348

Unit 13

1   square, circle, triangle, pentagon, rectangle, hexagon, pentagon, octagon

2   **3**   **4**   **5**

6   Answers depend on children's choices.

7

   isosceles   equilateral   scalene

8   Examples could include square, rectangle, parallelogram, trapezium, kite, rhombus

9   27

Unit 14

1

Name: cube	Name: cuboid	Name: cylinder	Name: square-based pyramid
Number of faces: 6	Number of faces: 6	Number of faces: 3	Number of faces: 5
Number of edges: 12	Number of edges: 12	Number of edges: 2	Number of edges: 8
Number of vertices: 8	Number of vertices: 8	Number of vertices: 0	Number of vertices: 5
Shape of faces: square	Shape of faces: 4 rectangles and 2 squares or 6 rectangles	Shape of faces: circles and rectangle	Shape of faces: triangles, square

2 Answers depend on children's choices. Example:

	Square faces	Not square faces
Prism	Cube	Cuboid
Not Prism	Square-based pyramid	Sphere

3 **a** cube   **b** square-based pyramid   **c** triangular prism   **d** cuboid   **e** tetrahedron

4 Possible answer: **5** Possible answer: **6** Possible answer:

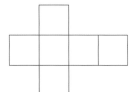
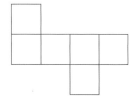

Unit 15

1

2 **1** West   **2** East   **3** West   **4** North   **5** South-west   **6** North-east   **7** North-west

3 $\frac{1}{2}$ clockwise turn, $\frac{1}{2}$ anticlockwise turn

4 $\frac{1}{4}$ anticlockwise turn, $\frac{3}{4}$ clockwise turn

5 $\frac{3}{4}$ clockwise turn, $\frac{1}{4}$ anticlockwise turn

6 **a** NE   **b** W   **c** NW   **d** SW   **e** E   **f** N   **g** S

7 Possible answers: **a** SE, NE   **b** E, W, NW, N   **c** S, E, N, W

8 Answers depend on the children's choices.

9 **a** SW   **b** NE   **c** S   **d** S   **e** S   **f** E   **g** N   **h** NE   **i** SE

Unit 16

1 Sensible estimates are acceptable.
    a 36, 16, 13, 5, 24, 27, 15, 10, 1, 18   **b** 165   **c** 12   **d** 17

    e dogs, cats, rabbits, hamsters

2 **a** 7   **b** 6   **c** 4   **d** 38   **e** 22   **f** first shop

3

Favourite colour	Symbols needed	Favourite colour	Symbols needed
Red	10	Yellow	$10\frac{1}{2}$
Blue	17	Orange	6
Black	5	White	4
Purple	$7\frac{1}{2}$		

   a Answers depend on children's choices.   **b** blue, yellow, red   **c** white, black, orange

4 **a** 12.30–1.15 p.m.   **b** 9.30–10.15 a.m.   **c** 25   **d** 15   **e** 15   **f** 155

Unit 17

1 £9.51	**5** 30	**9** 96	**12** 26p
2 £3.25	**6** 58	**10** £20	**13** £17.55
3 12	**7** 31	**11** 1.2 l or 1200 ml or	**14** £145.98
4 10	**8** 256	1 litre 200 ml	**15** £16.02

The UK's biggest home-learning range

These **WHSmith** Maths Practice Workbooks are available for **ages 7–11**

English titles are also available.

Your Learning Journey

The comprehensive range of **WHSmith** home-learning books forms a Learning Journey that supports children's education and helps to prepare for every success at school. We support children – and parents – through every step of that journey.

Practice – Reinforces classroom core skills

Challenge – Stretches more-able children

Progress – 10-minute progress checks

Revision – Develop skills for tests

Test – Practice for National Tests

Practice

The **WHSmith Practice Workbooks** for key stage 2 provide extra activities and support, building your child's confidence and understanding.

+ Plenty of practice to boost confidence
+ Master the core skills
+ More fun activities for you to work through at home
+ Written by experienced teachers
+ Complete with answers

For more information plus advice and support for parents visit www.whsmith.co.uk/readytoprogress

Shop online at whsmith.co.uk
WH Smith Retail Ltd SN3 3RX

ISBN 978-1-4441-8880-6